SITTIN' IN with the BIG BAND

Guitar

jazz ensemble play-along

	Page #	Demo track	Play-Along track
Vehicle	2	1	2
Sax to the Max	4	3	4
Nutcracker Rock	6	5	6
Fiesta Latina	8	7	8
Now What	10	9	10
Goodbye My Heart	12	11	12
Two and a Half Men	14	13	14
Burritos to Go	16	15	16
Drummin' Man	18	17	18
Swingin' Shanty	20	19	20
Play That Funky Music	22	21	22
Performance Notes	24		

How to Use This Book

Each arrangement has two CD tracks:
1) Demonstration track. The guitar part is in the mix. Listen to how your part is played by professional musicians to copy the comping style, rhythm, attack, phrasing, articulation, feel, style, and rhythm section blend.
2) Play-Along track. Your part has been taken out of the mix. You play-along with the big band.
3) See page 24 for Performance Notes.
4) There is a two-measure count-off click at the beginning of each play-along track.

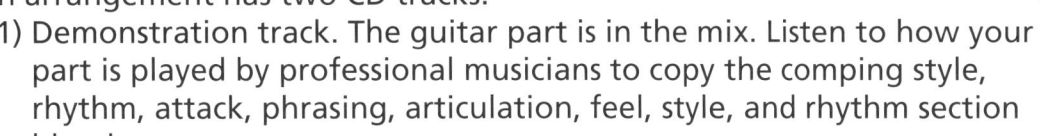

Alfred Publishing Co. Inc. thanks the students of
Mary Ward Catholic Secondary School Jazz Ensemble, Toronto, Canada,
John Volpe, director, Vince Gassi, assistant director, and photographers Jackie Fong and Jermaine Ong.

Alfred Publishing Co., Inc.
16320 Roscoe Blvd., Suite 100
P.O. Box 10003
Van Nuys, CA 91410-0003
alfred.com

A Division of ALFRED PUBLISHING CO., INC.
All Rights Reserved Including Public Performance

Any duplication, adaptation or arrangement of the compositions contained in this book requires the written consent of the Publisher.
No part of this book may be photocopied or reproduced in any way without permission.
Unauthorized uses are an infringement of the U.S. Copyright Act and are punishable by law.

ISBN-10: 0-7390-4519-9

SAX TO THE MAX

Guitar

by Mike Lewis

NUTCRACKER ROCK

Guitar

By TCHAIKOWSKY
Arranged by MIKE SMUKAL

FIESTA LATINA

Victor Lopez

NOW WHAT

By MIKE KAMUF

Guitar

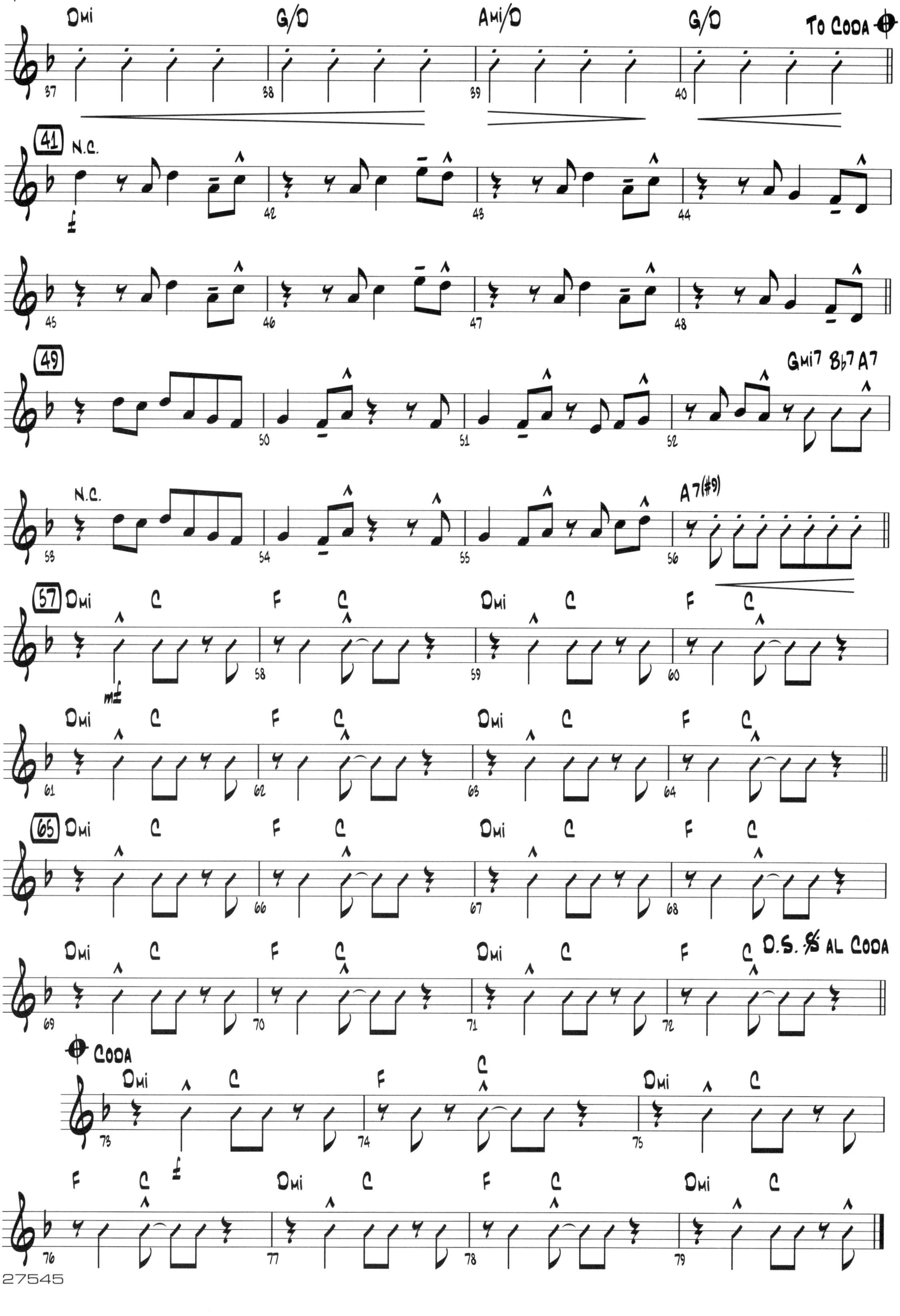
Dmi
G/D
Ami/D
G/D
To Coda
N.C.
Gmi7 Bb7 A7
N.C.
A7(#9)
Dmi
C
F
C
D.S. al Coda
Coda

PERFORMANCE NOTES FOR GUITAR

Playing guitar in a big band is challenging but very rewarding. Here are a few specific tips for playing guitar in a big band:

- Within the typical rhythm section, the guitar and piano must work especially close. Share the comping duties. Always be sensitive to blend with the rhythm section and the ensemble.
- "Comping" means to accompany or compliment. Always keep it simple, tasteful and supportive. Less is more.
- Various responsibilities for the guitarist are: comping, supporting the ensemble harmony and rhythms, playing individual lines with wind players, soloing, and supporting various soloists.
- Slash marks indicate to comp using three or four note chords usually in a quarter note rhythm pattern. Typically, the third and seventh are the most important notes in a seventh chord.
- Become skilled at reading both chord changes, written notes and creating chord voicings.
- Always be sensitive to your volume and sound. Begin by setting the tone controls on the amplifier to the mid-point and then adjust as needed. For a rock tune, the goal is to approximate an electric guitar sound, but for a jazz swing tune, strive for a hollow body jazz guitar sound with dark overtones. Listen to examples of these different types of instruments for reference.
- The guitar part is a guide and suggestion of what to play. Depending on your ability and experience, you can play the part as written or embellish but with good taste and musicality. Always listen!
- Generally, in a big band chart, when there is a written out part with no chord symbols, the arranger wishes the part played as written. When there are only chord changes and/or slashes, then comp in the style of the chart.
- For a sound that blends, consider using medium thickness picks which will give the sound a bright, acoustic quality and hold the pick loosely between the thumb and index finger.
- For a swing style comp of quarter notes, strum straight quarter notes trying to cut off (mute) the sound of the chord right after striking the strings. Strum from the elbow; giving a bright, swinging sound that propels the rhythm section forward.
- The guitarist's quarter note comping style should perfectly mesh so that the guitar and bass merge into one big sound.
- If the chord has extensions you don't recognize, play the third and seventh (sixth) of the chord.

There is a two-measure count-off click at the beginning of each play-along track

Vehicle:
1) A rock style chart, dig in and play more aggressively than usual and strive for a brighter sound, but don't overdo the volume.
2) The written comping rhythms are also played by the piano, so listen, blend and lock in the feel.
3) Measure 65 is a rubato trombone solo. In 66, the drumset plays a fill in-tempo to bring you in for the last two measures.

Sax to the Max:
1) In the introduction, play the written notes with the saxes and brass. Listen and blend.
2) This chart calls for basic comping in the jazz swing style. Play quarter notes with a muted sound.
3) If the chord has extensions you don't recognize, focus on the third and seventh of the chord.

Nutcracker Rock:
1) Play measures 5–8 with a bell-like sound—play it clear and let it ring.
2) Although this is a rock style chart, avoid a radical rock tone—blend.
3) At measure 37, listen and match the articulation and phrasing with the horn players.

Fiesta Latina:
1) Play the introduction as written while listening, blending, and phrasing with the piano.
2) At measure 17, comp as written. You can embellish but keep it simple. Listen to the demo track.
3) At measure 49, listen and match the articulation with the other instruments.
4) The repetition is what builds the intensity of a Latin groove but stay focused and maintain energy.

Now What:
1) For measures 1–33, play the written part with the horns but listen, blend, and match the articulation and phrasing.
2) Comp at measure 34 playing quarter notes.
3) Solo the second time at measure 54! Play the written solo or ad lib on the chord changes.

Goodbye My Heart:
1) In measures 1–4 and 69–72, play unison with the piano—listen and match the phrasing so it will sound like one person playing.
2) Comp the rest of the chart with sensitivity. Ballads look easy but require concentration!

Two and a Half Men:
1) Beginning in measure 5, the "and" of beat 4 is played short for this repeated lick. The tied note is not actually played. This is common notation in jazz music.
2) At measure 17, because the bass is playing in two, you can comp the chord changes in half notes instead of quarter notes but measure 20 should be quarter notes because of the four chords. Listen and experiment with various comping patterns.
3) Measure 45 begins a traditional quarter note swing comp.

Burritos to Go:
1) Match the articulation and phrasing with the saxes and piano at the beginning.
2) The note tied over the bar is not actually played. Listen to the demo track.
3) At measure 17, play the quarter notes short but not clipped.
4) The repetition is what builds the intensity of the groove but stay focused and maintain energy.
5) At measure 41, play this written line in unison with the other instruments. Listen, blend and match the articulation and phrasing.

Drummin' Man:
1) Experiment with different chord voicings but try to limit the chords to three or four notes to maintain transparency with the piano.
2) In this traditional swing chart, comp quarter notes in the Freddie Green style. Freddie Green was Count Basie's guitarist for many years and perfected a distinctive comping sound and style that was just loud enough to add some rhythmic attack and harmonic content to the bass line. Green's chord voicings were usually only three-note voicings using only root, third, and seventh with no chord extensions. Green's style is often described as being felt more than heard.

Swingin' Shanty:
1) This is a traditional swing comp.
2) At measure 71, play the written part in unison with the trombones and bass. Match the articulation and phrasing.

Play That Funky Music:
1) "NC" means no chord. Play the written part in unison with the ensemble.
2) Play the funky line at measure 3 together with the bass.
3) At measure 17, match the trombones with the sixteenth note figures.
4) You can voice the chord changes as desired. Always focus on the third and seventh of the chord.

Recorded at **Bias Recording Studios,** Springfield, VA
Bob Dawson, Engineer
Featuring the **Belwin Jazz Big Band, Pete BarenBregge,** Director.

Learn **jazz concepts, improvisation** and **sight reading** for all instruments from jazz legend **Bob Mintzer!**

Play Along Book & CDs

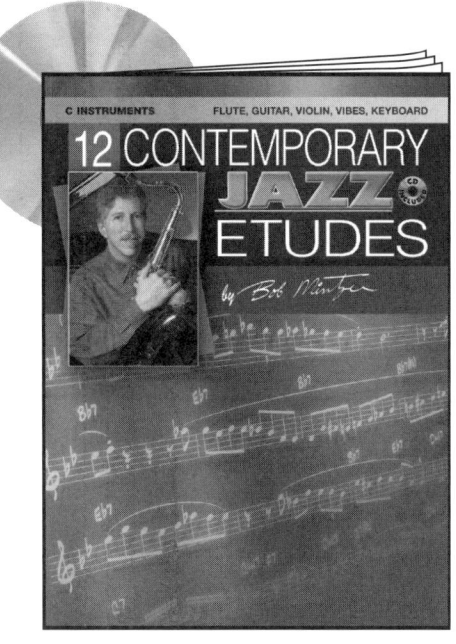

- 12 jazz etudes composed by Bob Mintzer in a variety of jazz styles, tempos, and time signatures
- Performance notes/tips for each etude to assist in interpretation and improvisation
- Play-along CD with a stellar rhythm section
- All books are compatible and written so they can be performed together!

12 Contemporary Jazz Etudes
Book & CD

(ELM04011)	C Instruments—Flute, Guitar, Violin, Keyboards	$24.95
(ELM04012)	B♭ Tenor Saxophone and Soprano Saxophone	$24.95
(ELM04013)	E♭ Instruments—Alto and Baritone Saxophone	$24.95
(ELM04014)	B♭ Trumpet and Clarinet	$24.95
(ELM04015)	Bass Clef Instruments—Trombone, Baritone, Horn and Tuba	$24.95

also available from Bob Mintzer and Belwin Jazz:

The Music of Bob Mintzer: Solo Transcriptions and Performing Artist Master Class CD
Book & CD

(0479B) $24.95

15 Easy Jazz, Blues & Funk Etudes
Book & CD

(ELM00029CD)	C Instruments—Flute, Guitar Keyboards	$19.95
(ELM00030CD)	B♭ Instruments Tenor Saxophone and Soprano Saxophone	$19.95
(ELM00031CD)	E♭ Instruments—Alto and Baritone Saxophone	$19.95
(ELM00033CD)	B♭ Trumpet and Clarinet	$19.95
(ELM00032CD)	Bass Clef Instruments—Trombone, Baritone, Horn and Tuba	$19.95

14 Blues & Funk Etudes
Book & CD

(EL9604CD)	C Instruments—Flute, Guitar Keyboards	$26.95
(EL9605CD)	B♭ Instruments Tenor Saxophone and Soprano Saxophone	$26.95
(EL9607CD)	E♭ Instruments—Alto and Baritone Saxophone	$26.95
(EL9606CD)	B♭ Trumpet	$26.95
(EL9608CD)	Bass Clef Instruments—Trombone, Baritone, Horn and Tuba	$26.95

14 Jazz & Funk Etudes
Book & CD

(EL03949)	C Instruments—Flute, Guitar Keyboards	$24.95
(EL03950)	B♭ Instruments Tenor Saxophone and Soprano Saxophone	$24.95
(EL03952)	E♭ Instruments—Alto and Baritone Saxophone	$24.95
(EL03951)	B♭ Trumpet	$24.95
(EL03953)	Bass Clef Instruments—Trombone, Baritone, Horn and Tuba	$24.95

Belwin JAZZ
*a division of **Alfred***

All prices in US Dollars and subject to change.
wo 53816

ORDER MUSIC TODAY

Learn what you need, play what you want.
OrderMusicToday.com

Jazz up your theory skills with
Alfred's Essentials of JAZZ THEORY

Written by renowned jazz educator and former IAJE President, Shelly Berg, this course is designed for students who have successfully completed one year of traditional music theory, or who are already familiar with basic theory concepts such as those taught in Books 1–3 of *Alfred's Essentials of Music Theory*.

Ideal for jazz enthusiasts & students alike!

Book 1 includes: Basic Elements (Melody, Harmony, Rhythm, Texture, Form) • Swing Feel, Swing Eighth Notes, Swing Groove • Syncopation, Bebop Style, Lick, Line & Melodic Soloing • Major Triad, Major Scale, Consonance • Major Seventh Chords, Chord Changes • Tonic Function, Scalar Melody, Passing & Neighboring Tones • Dissonant 4th and Resolution • Subdominant Major Seventh Chords, Voice Leading for Tonic & Subdominant Major Seventh Chords • Modes, Lydian Scale • Hierarchy of 3rd & 7th • Major 9th Chords, Major 6/9 Chords, Major Pentatonic Scale • Grace Notes, Scoops & Turns • Dominant 7th and 9th Chords, Dominant Function • Resolution of V7 Chords, Tendency Tones and Tritone • V7–I MA7 Common Tones and Voice Leading • Dominant Scale (Mixolydian), Bebop Dominant Scale • "Bluesy" Dominant Chords, Blue Notes, 12-Bar Blues Progression, Blues Scale • Glossary & Index of Terms & Symbols

Book 2 includes: Counterpoint-Bass and Melody • Walking Bass Lines • Walking Bass Lines in the Circle of Fifths, Two-Note Voicings • Comping & Comp Rhythms, Voice Leading • Brazilian Bass Lines & Comping Patterns • Minor 7th and 9th Chords & Inversions • Supertonic Function–iimi^7 and iimi^9 Chords • Resolution of iimi^7 to V7 • The ii-V-I Turnaround Progression • Jazz Language—Combined Scale / Arpeggio & "The ii-V Lick" • Jazz Language—Triplet Arpeggio & "The Bebop Dominant Lick"—Dominant 13th Chords & ii-V-I Voicings • Passing Minor +7 Chord & Progression • Tonicisation of the IV Chord • The ii-V Turnaround to IV • Melody for the Turnaround to IV • II Dominant Seventh Chords • ii^7 (#11) Chords, Lydian Dominant Scale, I Augmented Chord Extension (I+) • Diminished 7th Chords & Diminished Scales • Diminished 7th Function & Melodic Language • VI7 (♭9) Chord, The Turnback Progression • AABA Standard Song Form–"Take the A-Train" Progression • Jazz Language—Chromatic Leading Tones, Bebop Scales • Jazz Language—Auxiliary "Enclosure" Tones • The Jazz Blues Progression, Finding the Chromatics • Glossary & Index of Terms & Symbols.

Book 3 includes: Jazz Language—Melodic, Soloing & Melodic Sequence • Afro-Cuban Jazz—Clave & Tumbau • Afro-Cuban Jazz—Cascara & Montuno • Drop-Two Voicings • Minor 11th Chords & Sus Chords • Minor Tonic Chord, Jazz Minor Scale • Minor ii-V Turnaround, Half-Diminished Chord & V7 Chord • Resolutions and Voice Leading • Jazz Language—Scales for the Half-Diminished Chord • Jazz Language—Harmonic-Minor Scale & Lick for V7(♭9) • Turnaround to iv in Minor Keys • Minor Turnback, VI7-VI7(♭9)-i Cadence • Blues Scale in Minor Keys, Minor Pentatonic & Pentatonic / Blues Scales • Turnarounds to III, VI and VII in Minor Keys • Minor 12-bar Blues Progression • Minor Turnarounds in Major Keys—to ii and vi • Minor Turnaround in Major Keys—to iii, Deceptive Cadence (Backdoor Cadence) • Altered Dominant Chords • Jazz Language—Diminished Scale for Dominant Chords & Altered Dominant Cell • Jazz Language—Altered Dominant Lick and Scale • Step-Down Progression • IV-I (Plagal) Progressions, Backdoor Progressions • I-VI Progressions • ABAC Standard Song Form • Slash Chords • Glossary & Index of Terms & Symbols.

(00-20806)	Alfred's Essentials of Jazz Theory Book 1 & CD	$12.95
(00-20808)	Alfred's Essentials of Jazz Theory Book 2 & CD	$12.95
(00-20810)	Alfred's Essentials of Jazz Theory Book 3 & CD	$12.95
(00-20812)	Alfred's Essentials of Jazz Theory Complete (Books 1–3) & 3 CDs	$34.95
(00-22008)	Alfred's Essentials of Jazz Theory Teacher's Answer Key w/ 3 CDs	$37.50

Alfred Alfred Publishing Co., Inc.
P.O. Box 10003 • Van Nuys, CA 91419-0003
customerservice@alfred.com

Conquer theory fears with Alfred's
ESSENTIALS OF MUSIC THEORY

By Andrew Surmani, Karen Farnum Surmani, Morton Manus

The most complete music theory course ever!

This all-in-one series includes concise lessons with short exercises, ear-training activities and reviews. Available in three separate volumes or as a complete set, *Essentials of Music Theory* also includes Ear-Training CDs (performed by acoustic instruments), a Teacher's Answer Key Book, reproducible Teacher's Activity Kits, Bingo Games, Flash Cards and Computer Software. The Alto Clef edition includes primarily alto clef examples, with some treble and bass clef examples as well.

	Volume 1	Volume 2	Volume 3	Complete
BOOKS				
Student Book	(00-17231) $6.50	(00-17232) $6.50	(00-17233) $6.50	(00-17234) $12.50
Student Book w/2 Ear-Training CDs	—	—	—	(00-16486) $31.50
Student Book / Alto Clef (Viola) Edition	(00-18580) $6.50	(00-18581) $6.50	(00-18582) $6.50	(00-18583) $19.95
NEW! Student Book / Alto Clef w/2 Ear-Training CDs	—	—	—	(00-27642) $34.95
Teacher's Answer Key Book	—	—	—	(00-17256) $19.50
Teacher's Answer Key Book & 2 Ear-Training CDs	—	—	—	(00-17261) $37.50
EAR-TRAINING CDS				
Ear-Training CD		(00-17252) $10.95	(00-17253) $10.95	(00-17254) $18.95
DOUBLE BINGO GAMES				
NEW! Key Signature Double Bingo	—	—	—	(00-24448) $19.95
Note Naming Double Bingo	—	—	—	(00-19481) $19.95
Rhythm Double Bingo	—	—	—	(00-19479) $19.95
FLASH CARDS				
NEW! Key Signature Flash Cards	—	—	—	(00-24447) $9.95
Note Naming Flash Cards	—	—	—	(00-20320) $9.95
Rhythm Flash Cards	—	—	—	(00-19396) $9.95
TEACHER'S ACTIVITY KITS				
Teacher's Activity Kit	(00-19380) $19.95	(00-20373) $19.95	**NEW!** (00-26321) $19.95	**NEW!** (00-26327) $49.95
VERSION 2.0 SOFTWARE				
Student Version	(00-18827) $29.95	(00-20822) $39.95		(00-18833) $59.95
Educator Version	(00-18826) $99.95	(00-20821) $119.95		(00-18832) $199.95
Network Version (for 5 simultaneous users•)	(00-20322) $300.00	(00-20823) $350.00		(00-20321) $500.00

Which version do I need?

Student Version
- Ideal for individual students using the program one at a time
- Not necessary to track other users' progress

Educator Version
- Ideal for educators with one computer in a classroom, or for private lesson/studio use
- Educator has ability to track all users' progress & create custom tests

Network Version
- Includes all Educator Version features
- Designed for use on networked computers

•Additional Network User Licenses can be purchased as follows: **Volume 1–$20 each, Volumes 2 & 3–$25 each, Complete–$40 each**

Visit **alfred.com** and click on "Theory & Reference" for a handy interactive guide to help you decide which version is right for you.